SOCCER
Do You Know the Rules?

J. P. Verhees

In memory of my father.

The author wishes to express his special thanks to Paul S. De Moss and the other friends who helped with this project; and to Sharon Battles for her editorial assistance.

Published by The Soccer Book Company, Suite 285, 32 West Anapamu Street, Santa Barbara, California 93101

Cover design by Michael Beickel
Design and typography by Jim Cook/Santa Barbara

LIBRARY OF CONGRESS CATALOGING IN PUBLICATION DATA
Verhees, J.P. (Jean Paul), 1946–
   Soccer, do you know the rules?
   Includes index.
   Summary: Humorous illustrations with explanatory
text present the "Seventeen Rules of Soccer."
   1. Soccer—Rules—Juvenile literature. [1. Soccer—
Rules]   I. Title.
GV943.4.V47   1984   796.334'02'022   83-20440
ISBN 0-916019-00-4

Contents

*According to official international soccer rules (FIFA).

Introduction

In the course of coaching soccer in America and overseas, I became aware that no single book adequately explained the rules of soccer for teachers, parents, players, and spectators new to the game. Every time I saw an argument or confusion over rules, I became convinced that a book would have to be written to clarify the rules of soccer.

The primary aim of *Soccer: Do you know the rules?* is to explain in a simple and clear fashion the seventeen rules of soccer necessary to play a soccer match. I have strived for accuracy in paraphrasing the FIFA (the international governing board of soccer) rules. In some cases rules will vary locally. When in doubt, always check with your coach or the referee.

Michael Beickel's animated caricatures are a distinctive part of this work. The expression and movement of the illustrated players provide a unique insight into the rules. I am indebted to Michael's hard work and refreshing art—for three years we worked together to complete the project.

This book is for all ages and skill levels. My hope is that it will nurture a complete understanding of the rules so that the game can be played and enjoyed.

Thank you for the love of soccer!

Preface

In soccer there is an old saying that errors lead to goals. Indeed, if two teams are evenly matched, the winning goal frequently comes as a result of a playing error due to a misunderstanding.

An even greater area of misunderstanding is in the knowledge or lack thereof of the rules of soccer. Perhaps there is no other sport where the rules are more taken for granted.

JP Verhees, an accomplished player, teacher, author, and artist, has developed the first truly educational and entertaining approach to the rules of the game. On reading this book the reader will soon realize that the author has captured both the imagination and attention of soccer players from every walk of life. Players of every race and nation can identify with the "actors" featured in the pages of this book.

I encourage anyone and everyone associated with soccer to carry this book with them. It should be required reading for players, coaches, referees, and spectators. Moreover, it is a landmark effort which is much needed and long overdue. Bravo, JP Verhees!

C. CLIFFORD MCCRATH
*Soccer coach, Seattle Pacific University;
director, Northwest Soccer Camp; member,
NCAA Soccer Rules Committee.*

RULE 1
The Playing Field

THE GOAL POSTS

According to the International Federation of Football Associations (FIFA), the **goal posts** must be made of wood, metal, or another approved material, and painted white. Their width and depth may not be more than 5 inches (0-12cm). They may be square, rectangular, round, semi-circular, or elliptical.

If the cross bar is broken during a game and there is no material to replace it, the referee may end the game. If it is an informal game and both teams and the referee agree, a rope may be used as a cross bar if it is stretched tight enough for the ball to bounce off of it.

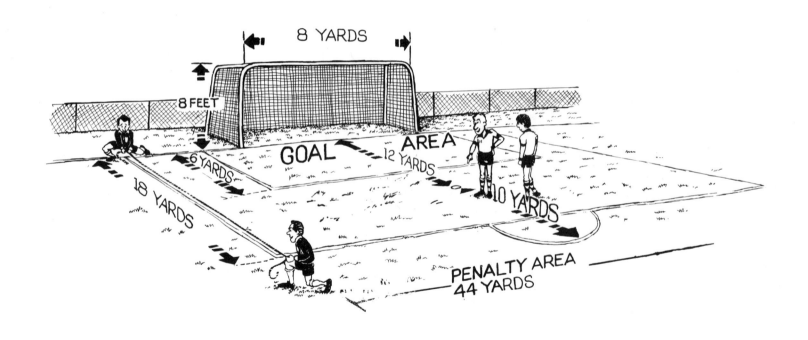

THE GOAL AREA

The **goal box** is 20 yards (18.32 meters) long and 7 yards (5.5 meters) wide. The **penalty box** area is 44 yards (40.32 meters) long and 18 yards (16.5 meters) wide. The distance between the goal line and the penalty box circle is 22 yards (20.15 meters).

THE PLAYING FIELD

The minimum length of a soccer field is 100 yards (90 meters). The maximum length of a field is 130 yards (120 meters).

The minimum width of a field is 50 yards (45 meters). The maximum width is 100 yards (90 meters).

The outside boundary lines on the sides are called touch lines. The outside lines beside the goals are called goal lines. The line at the halfway mark on the field is called the halfway line.

There is a center circle and a center spot.

At the corners of the field are the corner areas. They are one yard deep. Corner flags mark the corners of the field.

There are two goals, each with a goal area within a penalty area. Within the penalty area is a penalty spot, where the ball is placed when a penalty kick is awarded.

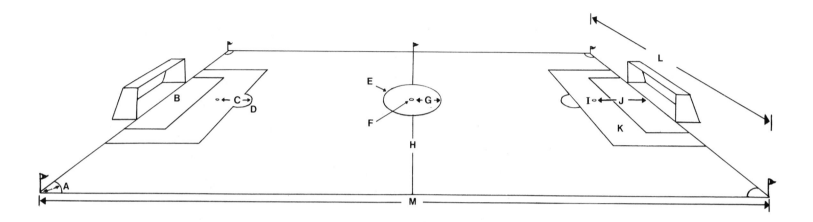

A. Corner Kick (3-foot [1 meter] arc)

B. Keeper's Box

C. 10 yards (9.15 meters)

D. Penalty Arc

E. Center Circle

F. Kick-Off Spot

G. 10 yards (9.15 meters)

H. Half or Offside Line

I. Penalty Spot

J. 12 Yards (11 meters)

K. Penalty Area

L. Max. width: 100 yards (90 meters)
   Min. width: 50 yards (45 meters)

M. Max. length: 130 yards (120 meters)
   Min. length: 100 yards (90 meters)

RULE 2
The Ball

The ball must be spherical.

It must have an outer surface of leather or other material approved by the international board. Materials that could be dangerous to players may not be used in making the ball.

An adult regulation ball may not be more than 28 inches (71cm) or less than 27 inches (68cm) in circumference. At the start of the game, the ball must weigh between 14 and 16 ounces (396-453 grams). The pressure must be 9.0-10.5 pounds per square inch at sea level.

Adults use a size 5 ball; younger players often prefer a size 4 or a size 3 ball, which are smaller than adult regulation balls.

RULE 3
Number of Players

A team may have only 11 players on the playing field. The goalkeeper, of course, is counted as one of the 11 team members.

A team must have at least 7 players to begin a game.

National youth leagues, schools, colleges, and other soccer groups vary on the number of substitute players allowed. Check with league rules for local interpretation.

The goalkeeper may be switched with another goalkeeper during the game if the referee agrees. Any player may be changed to a goalkeeper if the referee agrees.

RULE 4
Equipment

THE PLAYER'S EQUIPMENT

A player must wear a shirt, shorts, socks, and proper footwear. Many players use shin guards to protect the area below the knees.

A player may not wear any equipment that might be harmful to another player. Players are not allowed to wear: earrings, glasses, necklaces, wristwatches, bracelets, illegal spikes on shoes, or any cast, elbow or knee brace the referee considers dangerous; studs are permitted on the soles of the shoe if they are no longer than three-quarters of an inch, at least one half an inch in diameter, and must be rounded.

THE GOALKEEPER'S EQUIPMENT

A goalkeeper needs extra protection. He might prefer to wear long sleeves to protect his elbows; elbow pads are also helpful. He often wears knee pads to protect his knees. Gloves may be worn for a better grip on the ball. Caps may be worn to block the sun.

The color of the goalkeeper's uniform must contrast with all other uniforms on the field. He must not be mistaken for another player. When several players are trying to make a goal, the referee must be able to see who the goalkeeper is and who the players are.

RULE 5
The Referee

There are three officials who are responsible for controlling the game: *a referee* and *two linesmen*.

The referee is responsible for enforcing the rules of the game. He inspects the field and the players' equipment before the game, and makes sure everything is legal.

The referee keeps a record of the game. When a player makes a goal, the referee records the goal and the jersey number and name of player. The referee keeps track of who has received a yellow card (caution) and who has received a red card (ejection) indicating a foul.

The referee signals for the start and end of the game. The referee may stop the game at any time for an interference or an injury or any purpose he deems necessary.

The referee allows only coaches and trainers on the field, and only with his permission.

The referee gives warnings to players for misconduct. A player may be put out of the game by the referee for violent conduct, serious foul play, or abusive language.

The referee is the timekeeper.

When it is difficult to see because of fog, rain, or snow, the referee may suspend or terminate the game.

The referee may give warnings for misconduct to coaches, trainers, or players who are sitting on the sideline.

A player may not enter or leave the field without the referee's permission.

By convention, the captain is allowed to ask questions of the referee; however, there is no rule which prevents any player from speaking to the referee. The coach has no more right to do so than any player.

Yes, it is a goal if the ball bounces off the referee and goes into the goal.

RULE 6
The Linesmen

Because a referee cannot be everywhere at once, linesmen are necessary to help the referee control the game. The linesmen carry flags, make decisions, and inform the referee when a substitute wants to enter the game. They indicate when the ball is in or out of play on corner kicks, throw-ins, and goal kicks.

Linesmen are not the final authority. All final decisions are made by the referee.

RULE 7
The Duration of the Game

A regulation game is divided into two halves of 45 minutes duration, with a 10-15 minute halftime break.

If the game is delayed for any reason, such as an injury, the referee may add the lost time to the regulation game period. Players are not allowed to delay the game by kicking the ball out of play in order to gain time.

Game lengths vary for youth leagues, schools, colleges, and other soccer groups. Check with your local officials.

RULE 8
Start of Play

After a coin flip, the winner has the choice of kicking off or choosing which end of the field his team wishes to defend. All players must be on their own half of the field before the game begins. The opposing team must be at least 10 yards (9.15 meters) away from the ball, outside the center circle when play begins.

The referee must signal and blow the whistle before the game can start.

The ball must be kicked into the opposing team's half of the field. The player who has given the first kick may not touch the ball again until another player has touched it.

A goal may not be scored directly from a kick-off.

The official start of the play is after the ball has traveled its full circumference, or one turn of the ball.

RULE 9
Ball "In" and "Out" of Play

The ball is not out of bounds (out of play) until the *entire* ball has passed over the touch line or the goal line. If only half of the ball has crossed the line, it is still in play.

A player may go outside the lines to keep the ball in play.

A ball is still in play when it bounces off either a player, corner flag, goal post, or referee.

A drop ball occurs when the referee drops the ball between two opposing players. This restarts the game after the referee has purposely stopped the play for a non-penalty situation. A goal may be scored directly from a drop ball.

To put the ball back in play, a drop ball is given where the play is stopped or injury has occurred. The referee holds the ball a little below chest level and releases the ball.

A ball must touch the ground before either player may touch it. If a player touches the ball before it touches the ground, the referee will call it and the drop ball will be taken over.

RULE 10
Method of Scoring

A goal is scored when the ball completely passes over the goal line, between the goal posts, and below the crossbar—provided it has not been thrown, carried, or propelled by hand or arm of a player from the attacking side.

A goal may not be scored directly from a kick-off, a goal kick...

...or a throw-in.

But a goal may be scored from a punt.

A ball may be carried in by the chest.

A ball may be carried into the goal between the knees or feet.

Goals may not be scored directly from a kick-off, goal kick, or throw-in because a second player must touch the ball before it can be a goal.

The same rule applies if a goalkeeper makes a goal kick that sends the ball outside the penalty box and the wind blows the ball back into the goal. This is not a goal because the ball was not touched by a second player after it was kicked by the goalkeeper. The opposing team will be given a corner kick.

NOT OFFSIDE

OFFSIDE

RULE 11
Offside

A player is in an offside position if he is *ahead of the ball* and there are not two opponents closer to their own goal line than he is. This is illegal only if the player is participating in the play.

If a player is participating in the play, when does a referee determine that he is in an offside position? It is the position of the player *at the moment the ball is passed forward by a teammate* that must be judged, *not* his position at the time he receives the ball.

When the referee declares a player offside, an indirect free kick will be given to the opposing team at the point of the infringement.

A player is *not* declared offside if he receives the ball directly from a goal kick, corner kick, throw-in, or drop ball.

A player is *not* declared offside if he receives the ball after it bounces off a defender who was in control of the ball.

A player is *not* in an offside position when he is in his *own half* of the field of the play.

A player who receives the ball directly from a goal kick is not offside, even when the player is over the midfield line. She is offside if she receives the ball from a punt, which is not a restart of play.

This player will not be offside because she is receiving the ball on her own half of the field.

This player, taking the ball to the goal, will not be offside because a player cannot be offside on a drop ball.

This player will not be offside because a player cannot be offside when he receives the ball directly from a throw-in.

The player receiving the ball will not be offside because the ball has been deflected by the goalkeeper, who then becomes a defensive player.

This player will not be offside because a player cannot be offside if the
ball is received directly from a corner kick.

When a player shoots the ball and her teammate receives it after it hits a defender, the teammate should not be called offside. The teammate is not offside because *she was not participating in the play* when the ball was shot at the goal.

OFFSIDE:

The first player receiving the ball directly from a corner kick is not offside. If the receiving player passes to a teammate who is in an offside position, the teammate shall be called offside.

OFFSIDE:

A player who receives the ball from a throw-in is not offside. If the thrower moves into an offside position at the moment his teammate passes the ball to him, the thrower becomes offside.

OFFSIDE:

If a player in an offside position hinders the goalkeeper's vision while his teammate shoots at goal, the player is to be called offside.

OFFSIDE:

The player receiving the ball off the goal post is offside because she was in an offside position at the moment her teammate released the ball.

OFFSIDE:

This player receiving the ball from his teammate is offside because he is in line with a defender at the moment the ball is released.

OFFSIDE:

The player last receiving the ball here is offside.

NOT OFFSIDE:

When a defending player leaves the field of play and creates an offside situation for the opposing team, the player should be cautioned by the referee. In this instance, the goal is good.

NOT OFFSIDE:

The player receiving the ball is not offside because he did not move into this position until after the ball was passed by his teammate.

RULE 12
Fouls and Misconduct

A player who intentionally commits any of the following offenses [see Rule 13] shall be penalized by the referee giving a direct free kick to the opposing team from the place where the foul took place.

If an intentional foul is commited by a defender within the penalty area, the referee will give the opposing team a penalty kick instead of a direct free kick.

RULE 13
Free Kicks

There are two types of free kicks: (1) DIRECT, from which a goal may be scored without another player first touching the ball, and (2) INDIRECT, from which a goal may not be scored unless the ball has been played or touched by another player after the kick. All free kicks (except a penalty kick) are to be taken from the spot where the foul took place. The opposing team must be at least 10 yards away from the ball.

DIRECT FREE KICK

There are nine fouls which will result in a direct free kick.

1. Kicking an opponent is not allowed.

2. Jumping into an opponent is not allowed.

3. Tripping an opponent is not allowed.

4. Violently or dangerously charging an opponent is not allowed.

5. Charging an opponent from behind is not allowed.

6. Striking an opponent is not allowed.

7. Holding an opponent is not allowed.

8. Pushing an opponent is not allowed.

9. Handling the ball—carrying, striking, or propelling the ball with the hands or arms—is not allowed.

A hand-ball is when the ball is played intentionally by any part of a player's hand, elbow, or arm. It is not a hand-ball if the ball touches the *top of the shoulder*. Many times a referee will not call a hand-ball because he judges that a player does not intentionally touch the ball.

Obstruction is when a player deliberately blocks the progress of an opponent instead of playing the ball. The result is an indirect free kick for the other team.

INDIRECT FREE KICK

Any of the following five offenses will result in an indirect free kick being given.

1. Crouching to stop another player is not allowed.

2. A player is not allowed to *bend too low* and involve the opposing player in a dangerous play.

3. A player is not allowed to kick *too high* and involve the opposing player in a dangerous play.

4. Unsportsmanlike conduct is not allowed.

5. Charging the goalkeeper is not allowed.

RULE 14
The Penalty Kick

When a penalty kick is taken, all players except the kicker and the goal-keeper must be outside the 18-yard (16.5 meter) penalty area, and 10 yards (9.15 meters) away from the ball.

The goalkeeper must stand on his own goal line and not move his feet until the kick is taken.

A player is not allowed to tackle or charge the goalkeeper when the goalkeeper has the ball *in his possession* (both hands on the ball, or one hand if the ball is pinned to the ground or the body).

If the goalkeeper fouls an opponent within the penalty area, the referee will usually award a penalty kick.

When the ball is in play outside the penalty area, a penalty kick will be given if a foul occurs inside the penalty area.

During a free kick, defending players may make a wall and try to block the ball. If the defending player moves his arm and the ball is intentionally blocked or changes direction, the referee must call a handball and give a penalty kick. This is only if the foul occurs in the penalty area.

The defending male players making a wall are allowed to protect their groin; female players are allowed to cross their arms over their chests.

If the goal is not scored and the ball is deflected by the goalkeeper, the player who took the penalty kick may kick the ball again and try to score a goal.

If the ball bounces off the goal posts or the crossbar, it may not be kicked again by the player who took the penalty until it has been touched by a teammate or defending player. The goal would then count.

RULE 15
The Goal Kick

All opposing players must be outside the 18-yard (16.5 meter) penalty box. The goal kick is kicked by either a defending player or the goalkeeper from the goal area, and must be kicked beyond the penalty area to be in play again. The player who kicked the ball cannot touch the ball until another player has touched it.

During a goal kick, the goalkeeper or player is not allowed to hold the ball and delay the game. A goalkeeper is not allowed to take more than four steps before he releases the ball. A goalkeeper must kick the ball before he crosses the penalty-area line.

RULE 16
The Throw-In

When the ball goes over the touch line, a throw-in will be given to the opposing team.

The ball must be thrown in from over the head and with equal pressure from both hands. Both feet must be on the ground at the moment the ball is released.

A player must stand behind or on the touch line, but not over the line.

If the ball is not thrown in correctly, the referee will give the opposing team a throw-in.

RULE 17
Corner Kick

When a player kicks the ball over his own goal line, the opposing team will be given a corner kick.

When a player kicks the ball over the opposing team's goal line, the opposing team will be given a goal kick.

When the ball is in the corner ready to be kicked, all opposing players must remain 10 yards (9.15 meters) away from the ball until the ball has been played or traveled the distance of its circumference.

The ball must be within or on the lines of the corner flagpost area.

The flags posts that mark the
corner may be held during a
corner kick...

...but they may not be
removed.

When is a shoulder charge legal?

This is the only legal body contact that is not disallowed by the referee. It is made when both players use shoulders *evenly*. Each player presses his shoulder against the shoulder of the opposing player. If the legal shoulder charge is done correctly, it will not be called pushing, charging, or an obstruction by the referee.

What is a blocking tackle?

A player is allowed to jump straight up into the air behind the ball and make a screen with his feet—this is a legal blocking tackle. The defender does this to distract the opponent as he tries to take the ball away from the opponent.

A player is not allowed to jump toward the opposing player with two feet in the air to go for the player instead of the ball.

What is a sliding tackle?

A sliding tackle is taking the ball away from an opponent by sliding into the ball and kicking it away. Usually the legs are slightly bent; the heels should not rise higher than the ball so it does not become dangerous to another player. The sliding tackle can be done from behind, the side, or the front.

What is an advantage?

If the referee can see that to call a foul and stop the game would be a disadvantage to the team which has possession of the ball, an advantage is be applied.

If this happens in a game, the referee will call out "Play on!" This means he has seen the foul but is not going to stop the play because the team that would be given the free kick has the advantage of a passing or scoring opportunity. This rule helps to keep the game flowing.

There are cases where the referee will not call an advantage.

How is the ball headed?

Heading a ball is when a player tries to play the ball by hitting it with his head. If a player jumps to head a ball and happens to hit an opposing player on his way down, this will not be a foul.

If a player jumps *at* the
opposing player instead of going
for the ball, this will be a foul
(whether he gets the ball or not).

If a player holds an opposing player while heading the ball, he should be called for holding.

Who can best answer questions about soccer?

The best persons to answer questions about soccer are those who have played, coached, or officiated games. They should know the rules of the game. They also should know about conditioning, technique, tactics, and good sportsmanship. They know that most players who strive to improve can do so by practicing, watching better players play, and, of course, by reading books about soccer...like this one.

To order more copies...

Mail card to THE SOCCER BOOK CO., Suite 285, 32 W. Anapamu St., Santa Barbara, Calif. 93101, USA. Make check or money order payable to *The Soccer Book Co.*

Please send me _____ copies of SOCCER, DO YOU KNOW THE RULES?

I have enclosed $ _____ according to the schedule below.
(Check or money order, please—Calif. orders please add 6% sales tax.)

NAME _____

ADDRESS _____

CITY/STATE _____ ZIP _____

Rate Schedule

No. of Copies	Price	Postage & Handling
1-5	$6.95 ea.	add $1 per book
6-23	$5.95 ea.	add 50¢ per book
24-99	$4.95 ea.	add 25¢ per book
100+	$3.95 ea.	add 15¢ per book

To order more copies...

Mail card to THE SOCCER BOOK CO., Suite 285, 32 W. Anapamu St., Santa Barbara, Calif. 93101, USA. Make check or money order payable to *The Soccer Book Co.*

Please send me _____ copies of SOCCER, DO YOU KNOW THE RULES?

I have enclosed $ _____ according to the schedule below.
(Check or money order, please—Calif. orders please add 6% sales tax.)

NAME _____

ADDRESS _____

CITY/STATE _____ ZIP _____

Rate Schedule

No. of Copies	Price	Postage & Handling
1-5	$6.95 ea.	add $1 per book
6-23	$5.95 ea.	add 50¢ per book
24-99	$4.95 ea.	add 25¢ per book
100+	$3.95 ea.	add 15¢ per book